The REAL ESTATE

MILLIONAIRE

Beginners Quick Start Guide to Investing In Properties and Learn How to Achieve Financial Freedom

ALEX NKENCHOR UWAJEH

The Real Estate Millionaire - Beginners Quick Start Guide to Investing In Properties and **Learn How to Achieve Financial Freedom**

The REAL ESTATE MILLIONAIRE

CONTENTS

HOW TO INVEST IN
REAL ESTATE

If you look closely at how a number of millionaires made their wealth, you'll find the vast majority of them used real estate investment. What you may not realize is that there are several ways to invest in real estate to build wealth, generate passive income and gain equity at other people's expense.

Here is a quick breakdown of some different ways you can invest in real estate:

Long-Term Residential Rental Property

Buying a property and renting it out to a tenant can be an excellent way to build passive income. Ideally, the landlord should charge enough rent to cover the cost of your mortgage payments, taxes and any associated costs of maintaining the property.

The focus of long-term rental property investing is cash flow. The tenant goes to work every week to pay down your mortgage. Any profit you make can be put towards paying off the mortgage even faster and building your equity, or put towards other investments to keep building your portfolio. When the mortgage is paid off, the landlord receives all the rent paid by the tenant (minus any ongoing expenses) as passive income.

Renovating and Upgrading Properties

Buying an old 'fixer-upper' in a great location can be an excellent way to increase your property value. The idea is to find an undervalued home in need of renovation or repair and buy it cheap.

You work on renovating the property to improve its overall market value. In some cases it's also possible to increase the amount of rent you're able to charge tenants, which can also increase your cash flow over the long term.

Flipping Property for Profit

Flipping property for profit is very similar to what day traders do on the stock market. The objective is to buy real estate with the intention of selling it for a profit within a short period of time. The basis behind this type of real estate investment is to purchase an undervalued property or buy in a climbing market and sell when the price increases.

In some cases, you can increase your profits by undertaking some renovations or repairs to the property before selling it. The goal is to increase the value of the property with any repairs you complete so the sale price represents a good profit for you.

Keep in mind that you're not earning any rent while the property is empty, so you'll need to factor in the holding costs during the renovation period. You're responsible for keeping up with the mortgage repayments, insurance costs, utilities, and ongoing

renovation expenses. It's important to manage any contractors, time frames and payments well during the renovation, as your costs could blow out your entire budget if you're not careful.

Wholesaling Properties

Wholesaling real estate is the term used when an investor signs a purchase contract for a property and then sells the same home to another buyer. There is no need to do any repairs or maintenance on the home when you're wholesaling. Your job is to sell the same property to another interested buyer at a higher price than you signed for on the contract. In some cases, the person wholesaling the property never even buys the home, as the contract is assigned to the new purchaser.

On closing day, the new purchaser pays the full amount. The seller receives the amount

you paid on your original contract. You receive the difference between the new purchase price and the original selling price.

Commercial Property

Some property investors love to invest in commercial real estate and prefer it to residential real estate. Your tenants are often businesses or companies, instead of individual people, so the lease agreements are often set over a longer term. A commercial tenant is also sometimes required to pay for everything, including his or her own repairs and maintenance.

The rental returns can also be higher in some areas than residential rental properties. However, banks tend to set more stringent loan terms on commercial properties than you'll get on a residential home. Commercial loan terms tend to be shorter and interest rates tend to be higher than regular mortgages.

Investing in the Family Home

When most people think about investing in real estate, they immediately consider the more obvious options: flipping for profit or

becoming a landlord and charging a tenant rent to live in the property.

However, it's possible to generate plenty of profit from investing in your own family home, if you do it the right way. You can't charge rent for living in your own home, so cash flow isn't a consideration with this type of investment strategy.

Instead, your focus is on capital growth and equity building. Buying a home that needs a bit of renovation or some repairs can be a good way to improve the value while you're living there. When the renovations are complete you can sell the property. If you purchase a home to live in and you reside there for more than two years, the money you make when you sell the property is tax-free.

Real Estate Investment Trusts

Real estate investment trusts (REITs) are kind of like mutual funds for rental properties. If you don't like the idea or the hassle of being a landlord, then investing in a real estate investment trust could be a solution for you. The group buys or builds a block of apartments, condos, commercial projects, land, industrial buildings, or government buildings, and each individual investor owns a portion of the total value of the property.

The company operating the investment group manages everything to do with the apartments, including collecting rent, taking care of maintenance, and locating the right tenants. Any profits are passed on to the shareholders in the form of dividends.

Vacation Rentals

Investing in vacation rentals can be a great cash-flow generator for some investors. The objective is to buy a house in a popular tourist location and engage the services of a good property manager to take care of management.

The problem with vacation rentals is that any rental income you receive can be seasonal. You might earn significantly higher amounts of money during peak tourist seasons, but the house might remain empty in the off-season. You're expected to cover the costs of holding the property when the house isn't bringing in any rental income, so be sure to factor in plenty of vacancy time when you're doing your calculations.

Property Development

Developing property for profit can be extremely lucrative, but it's also a much higher risk investment for a small investor. Developing property also requires significantly more cash upfront before you realize any profits.

Most people are familiar with large property developments, such as building entire apartment blocks or condos. However, smaller property developments can also generate healthy profits too.

For example, you might find a run-down old single-family property in a very popular neighborhood on a large plot of land. You have the option of renovating and upgrading that property into a multi-family home. Alternatively, you might also consider developing the property by demolishing the original dwelling and constructing a brand new multi-family dwelling in its place.

CREATE A MILLION DOLLAR MONEY MAKING WINNING PLAN

There are multiple different strategies you can use to create a million dollar investment property portfolio. The key to creating the right real estate investment plan to suit you lies in knowing which strategy to use and when to use it.

There might be occasions where you need to  start small to build up some cash so you can work your way up to bigger projects. There may be times during your wealth creation plan where you need to flip a home to access some extra cash. There may be other times when it's far more profitable for you to keep a property for the cash flow generated by rental

income and to take advantage of associated tax deductions.

Your own personal moneymaking plan will depend heavily on your individual financial situation. You also want to revise your plan from time to time as your investment goals change.

Here are some things you should include in your own investment strategy:

Due Diligence

Every investing strategy needs to begin with due diligence. If you don't do your homework and spend time completing your research, you risk buying a dud property that costs you money, instead of generating a profit.

Your due diligence should include:

Full neighborhood research

- Comparative prices of neighboring properties
- Full property inspection
- Full project budget forecast
- Estimated cost of renovations
- Anticipated sale price of the property after renovations are complete
- Associated costs of the purchase, including closing costs
- Property taxes and insurance premiums
- Holding costs during the renovation process
- Sales costs and agents fees
- Correct investing structure to suit your goals

When you've spent time working through the project on paper, you should start to see whether it would be profitable or not. Be as accurate as you can during the due diligence

phase, as it could save you thousands of dollars later.

Exit Strategy

Your exit strategy is almost as important as your due diligence. You need to have a clear plan for what you're going to do with the property before you purchase it. Your exit strategy also needs to have a clear deadline to work towards.

For example, if your goal is to flip it for a profit within 4 months, that's your exit strategy for that property.

If your goal is to keep it as a rental home for cash flow purposes and then sell it after 5 years, that's your exit strategy for that property.

Structure

Developing the right structure for your investment property portfolio is crucial. Some people buy properties in their own name. However, there are times when it makes more sense to consider other structures.

For example, if you're investing with family members or in partnership with unrelated people, you may want to consider registering a company or trust structure. It's vital you speak with your accountant about the right structure to use for your investing goals.

Cashflow Forecasting

Create a spreadsheet and work out your exact costs for each property you purchase for your portfolio.

It's crucial to have a clear forecast for the costs associated with holding the property.

For example, if your strategy is to flip properties you need to have a forecast showing all your holding costs, including taxes, mortgage interest payments, renovation costs, and selling costs. If the total costs don't represent a profit on paper, you can adjust your strategy accordingly.

If your strategy is to hold the property for a longer time as a rental home, your forecast needs to include the rental income earned, minus all your holding costs and tax advantages up until the deadline for your exit strategy is reached. If the rental income doesn't cover all the costs associated with holding the property and it's generating a loss, you might want to adjust your strategy to flip that home, reduce your costs, or find ways to increase the rent until it's profitable again.

When you generate a clear forecast for each individual property, it makes it much clearer whether a particular home is worth flipping for the short-term profit or holding as a rental property for long term passive income.

Quotes and Estimates

Estimating the cost of renovations and repairs on a home can be tricky. You may feel as though you've estimated enough funds to cover your project, but the reality may be very different.

Where possible, shop around for quotes from suppliers for the items you'll need for your renovation. Ask for estimates from tradespeople for the work you want done.

Call a few different realtors and ask for an appraisal on the estimated sales price for the property if you were to complete renovations. Ask their advice on what things they think

could potentially help to improve the overall value of the home.

You can also ask for an estimated rental income for the property so you can work out your cash flow forecasting properly.

Investment Mortgage

If you're wholesaling properties with no intention of closing on them, you probably won't need to think about an investment mortgage. However, if you're flipping or holding the property over a length of time, it's likely you'll need an investment mortgage.

Always take the time to shop around with different lenders. Speak to mortgage brokers to see what loan types are available to you and what rates they can negotiate. Compare the differences in rates between a fixed and an adjustable loan and see how your payments differ with varying loan terms.

Compare the rates you're quoted and work out the repayments you're expected to pay each month.

Some lenders require larger deposits than others, so shop around until you find a bank that matches your needs. If you can't find a way to borrow all of the funds you need, you can always adjust your strategy to consider wholesaling properties to build up a larger deposit amount. The result is that you borrow less money. Some banks offer cheaper interest rates on low loan-to-value (LTV) ratios, so you could be saving money on your investment costs. A lower loan amount also reduces your repayments and helps make your holding costs easier to manage in the long run.

A Winning Advisory Team

Any successful property investor needs to build a solid team of advisers around them. Your advisory team should include:

A good accountant who excels with property tax deductions

A realtor who is highly familiar with the area you're investing in

A bank manager or mortgage broker willing to help you find competitive interest rates for investment mortgages

Good, reliable tradespeople who can complete renovation works within your deadlines

Re-Assessing Your Property Investment Strategy

Throughout your property investment journey, you'll find there are times when you need to re-assess your strategy. For example, when you're first starting out you might focus more on wholesaling or flipping properties to generate cash profits faster.

Over time your strategy may change to buying and holding properties in your portfolio for the long term as rental homes to generate passive income.

You might also mix and match your strategies from time to time to suit your financial goals. For example, you might switch to renovating, upgrading or maintaining properties to increase equity and to boost the rent you can charge your tenants.

Property Type

There may be times throughout your investment strategy when different types of homes may become more profitable than others.

For example, single-family homes may be more profitable if your goal is flipping, but

multi-family homes may be more profitable for generating passive rental income. Likewise, a condo in a great location might be more profitable for your strategy than a big home in a terrible location.

The key is to assess each individual property on its own merits as it relates to your overall investment strategy.

Wholesaling versus Flipping

Wholesaling properties can be a healthy way to get started in real estate investment using little or none of your own money. Your aim with wholesaling is to find undervalued properties and sell them to other buyers at a profit.

If you do your homework right, you should be able to assign your purchase contract to the new buyer with your profit margin built into the sale price.

Ideally, you can market the property so it sells to the new buyer without you having to close on the property at all. Once the property sells, the new buyer gains an asset, the seller gets the original asking price and you receive the profit for the margin between the two prices.

Wholesaling properties for profit can generate some handy extra cash that can be used as further deposits on your next property purchases, or put towards paying for renovations on your next fix-and-flip project.

Flipping versus Renting

Your initial cash flow forecasting may have shown that a particular home might be

an excellent fix-and-flip-for-profit project. However, after the renovations are complete you might find that the property's value didn't increase as much as you hoped. By the time you sell it, you might be lucky to break even on your costs.

Rather than sell it and gain no profits, you have the option of re-assessing your strategy. You could rent the property to tenants and recoup some of your costs over the next 12 months. If the property value starts increasing after 12 months, you can re-assess again and see whether it's worth flipping then.

The same principle is also true in reverse. You might buy a property and your cash flow forecasting shows that it should be a profitable rental home for passive income. However, the realtor may struggle to find tenants willing to pay the rental amount you're charging. If your property receives less rent than you initially

expected, it might become more profitable for you to flip it for the capital profit instead.

Capital Profit versus Cash Flow

Buying a property with the sole intention of flipping it for a profit can be a great way to generate cash. You buy the property cheap, fix it up a bit and sell it for a profit. However, once that property is sold it stops earning you money. It's also no longer a part of your investment property portfolio once it's sold.

By comparison, keeping selected properties and renting them out, as part of your overall property portfolio can be a strong wealth creation strategy for many people. The rental income generates passive income that pays down the investment mortgage over time and covers all the other associated costs of owning the property. The property value may also increase over time, further adding to your wealth creation strategies.

When you're working through your property investment strategy, it's important to work out whether a property is better of being sold to realize the profits in the short term or whether it's worth keeping it over the long term to capitalize on cash flow from rental income and tax deductions.

Always weigh up your options with each property in your portfolio and know when to hold or when to sell.

FINDING THE BEST INVESTMENT PROPERTY DEALS OR GREAT BARGAIN PROPERTIES

There are always lots of properties available for sale at any given time, but that doesn't mean they're the right ones for your investment portfolio. The key to finding the best investment property deals is to spend time doing your homework before you buy anything.

Foreclosures

When a homeowner can't keep up with mortgage repayments, the bank may choose to foreclose on the property and sell it to recoup their money. Buying a foreclosed property can

be a great way to get a good deal, sometimes saving you tens of thousands of dollars, as the sale price is often well below the value.

However, there are some things to watch for when buying foreclosed properties.

Problems with the Property

Before you buy a foreclosed home, be sure to complete a full property inspection. If the home is being foreclosed on, it's a signal that the previous owners were already in some financial difficulty and couldn't afford their repayments.

It's also likely they were unable to keep up with maintenance, upkeep and repairs on the property too, so you may be purchasing a poorly maintained home. Many foreclosed properties still contain

furniture, trash, clothes and other personal items the previous owners left behind.

Bad or Incomplete Renovations

The previous owners may have had great intentions for renovating the property before falling into financial hardship. Some foreclosed properties show signs of poorly completed renovations or incomplete projects in progress that will need to be addressed.

Neglect and Vandalism

Some people also take out their frustrations with the bank on the home itself. There are homeowners who will remove appliances or vandalize the property and leave it in a woeful state of disrepair. The yards may be overgrown or dead. There may be termite damage or leaks that haven't been repaired.

You may also find that a foreclosed property may have been abandoned and left sitting vacant for a period of time, which increases the chance of vandalism and criminal activity. The property may have broken windows, graffiti, fire or water damage, or other damage that will need to be repaired.

No Seller Disclosure

As no one from the bank has lived in the house, they're not likely to have any prior knowledge of existing problems within the property. It's your job as the buyer to uncover any problems yourself during your due diligence.

Despite potential problems with the home, foreclosures can still represent a good deal for your property investment strategy. If you're willing to fix any problems and repair any damage to the home, you're likely to buy a home at a significant discount.

Tax Liens

Buying a home in a tax lien sale can mean getting a property at a great discount.

As homeowners fall into financial hardship, the chances of the property taxes going unpaid increases. Many states will use tax lien sales to force homeowners to pay their unpaid property taxes. Investors place a bid on the property to purchase the tax lien. Whoever bids the most cash for the tax lien wins the auction.

The tax collector takes payment for the unpaid property taxes out of the winning bid. In exchange, the winning bidder receives a lien over the property.

For property investors, there are two ways to receive a return on your investment. You can either:

1. You earn interest on your bid amount, or

2. You gain ownership of the property at a discounted price

Interest on your Bid

You submit a bid for the tax lien and it's the winning bid. If the homeowner can manage to find enough cash to pay their overdue taxes within the timeframe specified, then you get your investment amount back, plus an amount of interest paid on top of your original amount. In some states, the average interest paid on tax lien bids is around 10% to 12%, although some states pay higher.

For example, let's assume that a homeowner owed $500 in unpaid property taxes. You place a bid for $5,000 for that tax lien at auction. The homeowner has 12 months to

find enough cash to pay the full amount outstanding to redeem the lien. However, the amount outstanding is now much higher than the original $500 owed.

The homeowner now has to pay the original $500 in unpaid taxes, plus a 10% penalty. The owner is also required to pay 10% on the amount of the winning bid that exceeds the original bill.

So if the winning bid is $5,000 and the original bill is $500, then the amount that interest is charged on is $4,500. The homeowner needs to pay 10% of $4,500, which is $450.

If yours was the winning bid, you receive your $5,000 initial investment back, plus the $450 penalty interest fee.

Ownership of the Property

If the homeowner can't redeem their property within the timeframe specified, you have the right to file a lawsuit seeking the title to the property. Once the lawsuit is complete, you are the new owner of that home.

The legal process can be time-consuming and complex, but if your winning bid was just $5,000, then you've managed to purchase a property at a significantly discounted rate. It's strongly advised to ask lots of questions from your advisory team and do all your due diligence before jumping into tax lien investments.

LOCATION, LOCATION, LOCATION

Have you ever heard the saying "buy the worst house on the best street?"

Perhaps you've heard the more popular saying that buying property is all about "location, location, location?"

There's no point in buying a bargain property that's located in an area no one wants to buy in.

Choosing a good location for your investment property is all about understanding the demographics in a particular area. You want to find homes that are in desirable locations that increase the number of buyers willing to inspect the property.

Ideally, buyers look for prime properties in areas that give them easy access to the lifestyle and work amenities they need. For example:

- Close to good quality schools
- Homes with a great view
- Houses near entertainment or shopping outlets
- Easy commuting distance to work
- Economically stable areas
- Close to transport, health care and other public amenities

When you're searching for properties, it's a good idea to create a checklist of things in and around a particular location that suit your strategy. You might also want to include a list of bad or undesirable location items too.

Examples of undesirable locations for residential property investments include:

- ✖ Close to industrial or commercial areas
- ✖ Near railroad tracks or under flight paths
- ✖ In neighborhoods with high crime rates
- ✖ Economically depressed areas
- ✖ Close to hazards (e.g. nuclear power plant, electricity transformers, landfill, swampland etc.)

USING OTHER PEOPLE'S MONEY FOR YOUR INVESTMENTS

One of the best things about investing in real estate is that you can build your investment portfolio using other people's money (OPM).

There are lots of different sources of OPM you can take advantage of, but perhaps the two easiest options are:

- The bank's money
- Your tenant's money

If you intend on buying long-term rental properties, you might also get some benefit from tax deductions, so you can take advantage of the taxman's money too.

Let's look at the two easiest options for using other people's money to build your investment portfolio.

Leveraging the Bank's Money for Your Investments

There's no need to try and save enough cash to pay for your investment property out of your own pocket, especially when banks are willing to lend you money to complete the purchase.

The lender agrees to give you a loan for a fixed rate of return in exchange for collateral security, which is usually the asset for which the loan is being taken out. You sign the mortgage documents declaring you'll pay back the amount of money you borrowed, plus the interest charges due.

Building Wealth with Your Tenant's Money

If you're borrowing money to buy a long-term rental property, the borrowing criteria is pretty straightforward. The lender assesses your capacity to repay the loan based on your current income and debt levels. The lender also adds the rental income you earn onto your earned income, which increases your borrowing capacity a little further.

When the sale closes and your tenants move in, the bank has effectively given you the majority of the money to purchase the property. The tenants then go to work each week so they can afford to pay rent. The rent you earn should pay for all the ongoing costs associated with owning the property, as well as paying off your mortgage over a period of time.

Creating Down-Payments with Other People's Money

Let's assume you don't have a family home yet and you don't have any savings to use for a down payment on an investment property. You're starting from absolute scratch, so you'll need a way to build up enough cash to get into the property market.

You have several options available to you. You can:

■Save money over time out of your earned income
■Borrow money from family or friends to get started
■Find investors willing to fund your investment strategies
■Generate profits with real estate wholesaling

■Fix and flip real estate for profit

Trying to save for a home deposit from your own income is time-consuming, but it's always a good idea to have a buffer of savings in reserve if you're planning to enter the real estate market.

However, the plan here is to use other people's money where possible, so let's look at those options.

If you have a family member who is willing to lend you a down payment to get started, you can complete a fix-and-flip project. Once the property sells, you return the money you borrowed and keep any remaining profit to put towards your next project.

It may also be possible to find investors willing to put some money towards funding your investment strategies. For example, your investor puts money towards the down

payment, while you complete the due diligence and renovations on the property. When the property sells, your investor gets the initial investment back, plus a share of the profits. You keep the remaining profits to put towards more projects.

Wholesaling properties can be a handy way to generate enough cash for a down payment. You sign a purchase contract on a property and then assign that contract to another buyer for a profit. Your challenge is to find properties that you can sell immediately without closing on the home first.

Buying Investment Properties with No Money Down

In some cases, you will need to have a down payment in cash to complete the purchase for an investment property. However, there are still ways available where you can borrow the

entire cost of your investment property without any money out of your own pocket.

You see, banks will happily use the available equity in your family home as collateral security for the purchase of your investment property – but only if you approach the loan application correctly.

The process is called cross-collateralization. The bank uses your family home as security, but doesn't change the existing loan amount you have outstanding on your house. The bank then factors in the value of the investment property you want to buy and lends you money to cover the purchase price and closing costs of the home.

For example:

Let's assume the value of your family home is $300,000 and your remaining mortgage is just $100,000. You want to buy an investment property for $220,000. For the purposes of this

example, we'll assume you have $8,000 in closing fees, so you want to borrow $228,000 to purchase your investment property.

	Property Value	Debt Amount
Family Home	**$300,000**	**$100,000**
Investment Property	**$220,000**	**$228,000**
Totals	**$520,000**	**$328,000**

At first glance, it appears that your investment mortgage is 'underwater'. You owe more money on the property than it's worth.

However, the way the bank sees it, they have $520,000 worth of assets as collateral for your loans. In total, they only have $328,000 in

debt over both of your properties. That's a 63.07% loan-to-value (LTV) ratio overall.

Effectively, the bank's money has paid for you to own an investment property. Your tenant's money will eventually pay it off for you.

Building a $1 Million Investment Portfolio with OPM

Based on the previous examples, you should start to see how it's possible to build a strong portfolio using very little of your own money. However, once you get started it's easy to keep leveraging your assets to keep building more wealth.

The bank pays for the purchase and the tenant pays off the debt. If you buy an investment property that can be improved with some repairs and renovations, you also have the opportunity to increase the property's value further. As the property value increases, the

amount of equity you have available to leverage also increases.

For example, let's assume you purchased an investment property for $220,000 and also borrowed $8,000 to cover your closing costs. Let's also assume you spent a bit of time giving the property a fresh coat of paint, did some simple repairs, and spruced up the yards and landscaping before the tenants moved in. Fortunately for you, there are great tenants in the property who look after it well, so it looks in great condition.

For the purposes of this example, let's assume the value of the investment property has increased to $260,000 after your simple renovations and repairs. Let's also assume you've been slowly fixing up your own family home at the same time, so the value of your house has also increased to $320,000.

	Property Value	Debt Amount
Family Home	$320,000	$100,000
Investment Property	$260,000	$228,000
Totals	**$580,000**	**$328,000**

Remember, the bank doesn't know the value of your properties has changed yet.

In order to leverage that increase in equity to keep building your portfolio, you need to let the bank know about it.

Let's assume you find another excellent property that would be a great addition to your

investment portfolio. The purchase price is $235,000. Your closing costs are $8,500, so you'll need to borrow $243,500.

For this second investment property, you also want to upgrade the kitchen and complete some simple renovations to convert the basement into a teenager's retreat and laundry room that will cost you a total of $20,000, so add those costs to the mortgage as well. Your total borrowing amount is now $263,500 for the original purchase price of $235,000.

As part of your mortgage application for the purchase of your next investment property, you need to ask the bank to re-appraise your existing properties.

The bank adjusts the values on your collateral files, which increases the amount of equity you have available to leverage.

It also gives you sufficient equity to purchase your next investment property with no money down.

	Property Value	Debt Amount
Family Home	$320,000	$100,000
Investment Property 1	$260,000	$228,000
Investment Property 2	$235,000	$263,500
Totals	$815,000	$591,500

So far we've created a real estate portfolio of $815,000 and you still haven't used any of your own money. You're still using the bank's

money to buy assets, and your tenant's money is paying down your investment debts to create your wealth.

But the purpose of this exercise was to create a $1 million real estate investment portfolio, so let's leverage your assets a little further.

In the last example, the bank didn't increase the value of your second investment property, as their appraiser figured that the renovations weren't completed yet. As a result, the appraisal value on the bank's file still says the property's value is $235,000. However, your renovations have added another $30,000 to the value.

It's time to buy another long-term rental property…

This time the property costs $215,000 to purchase. Your closing costs are $8,000, so you're borrowing $223,000.

	Property Value	Debt Amount
Family Home	$320,000	$100,000
Investment Property 1	$260,000	$228,000
Investment Property 2	$265,000	$263,500
Investment Property 3	$215,000	$223,000
Totals	**$1,060,000**	**$814,500**

There you have it. You are the proud owner of $1.06 million worth of real estate.

Okay, it's true you owe the bank more than $814,000 – but don't forget that your tenants

are paying down those investment loans. Your focus is to repay the mortgage on your family home.

In fact, the mortgage on your family home hasn't changed throughout all of these examples, so you're in the same position as you were before you started investing.

The difference now is that you have investment debts that are being paid by other people and assets that are increasing in value over time.

Imagine if you owned those properties outright with no debts remaining. The rental income becomes your passive income every month. You no longer have loan repayments to worry about.

So, how can you start paying down those debts so you own your investment assets outright?

By fixing and flipping properties for profit...

FLIPPING PROPERTIES
FOR PROFITS

 Making money flipping properties can sometimes be more challenging than it looks. It's surprising how many people think it's as easy as buying a house, doing some simple painting or yard clearing, and then putting it back on the market at a higher selling price.

In reality, flipping property successfully requires careful planning.

Due Diligence

Before you buy any property at all, it's important to do your due diligence.

Check that you're really paying a bargain price for the house by comparing it

to other sales of similar homes in the same area

☐ Complete a full property inspection

☐ Assess the amount of work that needs to be done

☐ Get accurate quotes from tradespeople and suppliers for the materials and work you need done

☐ Get appraisals from trusted realtors for the estimated sale price of the home after renovations are complete

☐ Set an exit strategy deadline and ensure all work that needs to be done can be completed on time

☐ Create a cash flow forecast to estimate all your costs throughout the project

Finding the Right Properties

Not every property will be suitable for your investment needs. Some properties may already have extensive renovations completed. Others may be so far beyond help that no amount of rehab work can help them.

You might find plenty of properties out there that seem promising, but won't fit within your due diligence checklists or your cash flow forecast needs.

You'll also find some properties may not be priced reasonably enough to represent a profit once you add the cost of mortgage interest,

closing costs, renovation expenses, marketing and selling costs, and insurance premiums.

The key is to keep searching through multiple properties until you find one that fits your investment strategy perfectly. After all, there are always plenty to choose from, so there's no point rushing into a project that could end up losing money.

Keep searching until you find the right home in the right location to suit your needs.

Negotiating Price

When you've completed your due diligence checklist, it's time to negotiate your purchase price. You should already know approximately what the home would be worth by the time your renovations are complete and you should already have estimated figures for the cost of renovations, plus holding costs.

Your task is to negotiate a fair purchase price that allows you to realize a profit when you sell the home.

All too often people forget that negotiating is actually about striking a deal. Both the buyer and the seller want to achieve a happy outcome.

The seller needs the cash and the buyer doesn't want to pay any more than necessary. You both have certain expectations, so try to achieve a win-win outcome where the seller is happy and you get a reasonable price.

For example, if the asking price for the property you want is set at $240,000 and you don't want to pay any more than $200,000, perhaps begin your negotiations at $180,000.

The seller may counter your original offer and drop the price down to $230,000. You have the right to reject that offer and submit a new offer at $185,000.

The seller can continue negotiations with you until you both reach a mutually agreeable price.

Alternatively, the seller may also choose not to accept any further offers below their preferred sale price. For example, if the seller also has to repay a mortgage and still owes the bank $210,000, he may decide not to accept any offers below that amount of money.

If the amount is higher than your due diligence and cash flow forecasts allow for, walk away from the deal and find another property that fits within your strategy.

Always consider the seller's perspective when submitting your offers. Then work out the maximum amount you're willing to pay and stick to your budget.

Completing Renovations

It's surprising how many people believe they can complete most of the renovation work themselves in their spare time. What you may not realize is that trying to complete the whole reno project yourself could be costing you money in the long run.

It's common for people to start a flip-for-profit project with the intention of doing all the renovations and repairs on their own on weekends or after work. In reality, the time frame for the project extends out far longer than you might have planned for.

Rather than saving money on trades and labor costs, you're incurring additional costs on mortgage interest, insurance premiums, property taxes and utilities for the property. In

the end, you could end up spending far more than you budgeted for.

Ask for quotes from tradespeople who can complete the work that needs to be done before your exit strategy deadline. Work through your cash flow forecast carefully and decide whether the benefit of having work completed professionally and quickly is cheaper than holding the property over the longer term.

Curb appeal is another important factor with any renovation project. If the front of the home and the yards aren't appealing as a buyer drives up to the property for the first time, no one will want to go inside to look at the awesome renovations you've just completed.

Check that the landscaping is neat and lawns are mowed. Trim back any bushes or trees that look overgrown. Touch up any areas of paint and clean the driveway, porches and exterior walls.

You only get one shot to make a great first impression, so make it a good one.

Pricing Your Property

Choosing the right listing price is one of the most important tips for selling any home quickly. If your home is priced too low, you're leaving money on the table. However, if your price is too high the property could get stale on the market due to lack of interest.

You should already have spoken with a few different realtors about your property and discussed pricing during your due diligence. Double check what those same realtors think

about the proposed pricing after the renovations are complete.

Finding Buyers and Marketing

Once the renovations and repairs on the home are complete, you'll need to sell the property to realize your profits. Marketing your property is an important aspect of closing the sale quickly.

When it's time to think about marketing, compare how similar properties in the same area are presented. Consider what the advertised price is on those properties and make a list of any standout features your home has compared to those.

Take a closer look at your project budget and see if you have any surplus remaining to engage the services of a professional property staging company. A staging company dresses

the house to highlight its features and enhance its buyer appeal.

The staging company may temporarily furnish the house with strategically chosen furnishings designed to make each room feel more spacious and welcoming, which can help to improve buyer interest in the home.

When the home is dressed to impress, have some professional photos taken of the interior and exterior of the property. Those photos will become a strong selling point during your marketing campaign.

During your due diligence you should already have discussed the property at length with several realtors and selling agents. You should already have included the cost of their selling services in your cash flow forecast, so contact the agent and list the property as being on the market.

Double-check what advertising measures the agent intends on using. If the plan is to upload one or two photos and basic description on a real estate sales website, encourage the agent to use some of the professional photos you had taken to highlight the features of the home.

You should also give the agent the checklist you created that makes your home stand out from the competition in the area and work those features into the property description.

More buyers search for properties online than any other source. If your sales listing has only one or two basic photos and a bland description, you could potentially be losing a sale.

Take advantage of the Internet and let potential buyers see what the property is like while they're searching online. If you can generate interest while they're browsing the Internet, they're far more likely to turn up to inspect the property in person.

RISKS OF REAL ESTATE INVESTING AND INTEREST RATES

Every investment contains an element of risk. Even really good investments still have an inherent risk factor.

Your job as a real estate investor is to mitigate those risks by doing your homework properly before jumping into any deal.

Interest Rates

Many real estate investors are happy to sign on for a fixed interest rate mortgage over the long term. The primary benefit of a fixed rate mortgage is that you always know exactly how much your mortgage repayments will be. They won't change for the duration of the fixed term.

If your investment strategy is to buy long-term rental properties, you know your repayments are fixed. Of course, you have the benefit of being able to increase your rent each year, which increases your cash flow for that property.

However, some banks may charge penalty fees for breaking out of a fixed interest rate loan when you go to sell the property. Always check whether your lender charges a penalty fee for breaking out of a fixed term loan and factor those costs into your cash flow forecasts.

By comparison, the interest rate on an adjustable rate mortgage can fluctuate with the market. Adjustable rate mortgages are also commonly cheaper than their fixed counterparts, so your repayments may start out lower while interest rates are low. When interest rates go up, your repayments will

increase, which can impact your cash flow dramatically.

Over-Capitalizing

If you pay more money on your property than it's worth, you're over-capitalizing on your investment. Overpaying on the purchase price is often a sign the investor hasn't done enough due diligence or market research into property prices in the area. Always obtain a third-party appraisal to ensure you're not paying more than you should.

Blowing the Budget

Many real estate investors fail to maintain enough money in cash reserves to cover costs. This is especially true in fix-and-flip projects, where the investor must cover the cost of mortgage interest, insurance premiums, utilities, and ongoing renovation costs.

Be cautious about itemizing all of your costs and expenses as you incur them and always know what budget you're working towards. Where possible, try to ensure you have a buffer of surplus cash on hand to cover any contingency costs you didn't anticipate.

Bad Tenants

 Yes, it's true. There are plenty of horror stories out there about bad tenants trashing the landlord's property, vandalizing the home, removing fixtures and fittings before vanishing without a trace, and not paying rent.

Bad tenants are a risk every landlord takes. However, you can mitigate that risk by ensuring you, or your rental agent, complete background checks on every tenant.

Screen every application thoroughly and call their references. It also pays to check their credit score, as this can give you an indication what their past history with financial responsibility is like.

You can also ensure you have good insurance coverage for your rental property and stay up to date with the premiums. In the event that your property is damaged, your insurance policy should cover most – if not all – of the repairs. Some policies may even cover you for lost rent during the repair process. The insurance premiums are tax deductible anyway, so shop around and find the right level of coverage to reduce your risk.

TAKING ADVANTAGE OF
TAX BREAKS

One of the nice benefits of owing a rental property is that you can take advantage of some of the tax breaks available.  Paying less tax means more disposable income in your pocket overall from your earned income.

Landlord's tax deductions can really add up in your favor, if you know what you're able to claim and what you can't. Some of the things you might be able to deduct for owning a rental property might include:

Operating Costs

Your mortgage interest costs and any operating expenses you incur through owning a rental property are tax-deductible expenses.

In some cases, you may even be able to depreciate the cost of the property, even as the value starts to increase.

Repairs and Improvements

Any repairs to existing fixtures can often be deducted in the year you completed the project. However, any property improvements you make to the property may be depreciated over time instead of being instantly deductible.

Travel Costs

Some landlords aren't aware that they can deduct travel expenses associated with a rental property. Driving across town could mean deducting the cost of gas, tolls and parking. If you're flying across the country for rental property purposes, the cost of overnight accommodation, airfare, and a portion of your meals costs might also be deductible.

Home Office Expenses

If you operate your rental property business from home, it may be possible to deduct some of your expenses. Home office deductions can really add up, especially if you have a dedicated workspace set aside in the home. You might be able to deduct a portion of your utilities costs, homeowner's insurance premiums, Internet or phone expenses, and even a percentage of the interest you pay on your home mortgage.

Unexpected Losses

If your rental property is damaged or destroyed, you might be able to deduct some of the loss generated by the event. In most cases, insurance should cover some of your costs, but any losses you incur could be deductible.

Tax Credits on Historic Properties

If your rental property is considered an historic property, you may be able to take advantage of tax credits on federal income taxes. Some states may also offer tax credits on state income taxes for rehabilitating historic properties.

Deferring Tax Payments

There are specific instances where you might be able to put off paying taxes on a rental property you sell. The IRS calls this a 'Section 1031 exchange', which lets you sell a property that has appreciated in value, but only as long as you purchase another rental property in a like-kind transaction.

To make it easier to track your investment-related expenses, it's a good idea to operate

separate accounts for your rental activity. For example, separate bank accounts; mortgage accounts or credit cards make it easier to ensure you track rental business spending separately from any personal spending.

It's also a good idea to keep track of any receipts or invoices related to your rental property throughout the year. Enter the amounts you spend into a spreadsheet to make it easier to keep track of your costs at tax time.

To ensure you maximize the taxation benefits available for being a landlord, be sure to discuss your rental property and associated expenses with a good accountant.

CONCLUSION

Investing in real estate is an exciting way to build wealth. There are always so many options and strategies to choose from, that can help to build your portfolio.

The real key behind the success of any real estate investment is doing your homework. There is no short cut to success with property. It's all about putting in the effort and creating a strong strategy that works for your individual situation.

Spend time going over the numbers. Research the market. Work through your budget. Know your intended buyer or tenant before you begin. Ask lots of questions from your

accountant, your realtor, your tradespeople, your bank manager or mortgage broker, and really listen to the responses you get.

Before long, you'll be building wealth with your own investment property portfolio.

Check Out Other Books:

- **In The** Pursuit of Wisdom: **The Principal Thing**

- **Investing in** Gold and Silver **Bullion - The Ultimate Safe Haven Investments**

- Nigerian Stock Market Investment: **2 Books with Bonus Content**

- **The** Dividend Millionaire: **Investing for Income and Winning in the Stock Market**

- **Economic Crisis: Surviving Global Currency Collapse - Safeguard Your** Financial Future with Silver and Gold

- Passionate about Stock Investing**: The Quick Guide to Investing in the Stock Market**

- **Guide to Investing in the Nigerian Stock Market**

- Building Wealth with **Dividend Stocks in the** Nigerian Stock Market **(Dividends - Stocks Secret Weapon)**

- **Beginners Basic Guide to Investing in Gold and Silver Boxed Set**

- **Beginners Basic Guide to Stock Market Investment Boxed Set**

- Precious Metals Investing **For Beginners: The Quick Guide to Platinum and Palladium**

- Bitcoin and Digital Currency for Beginners: The Basic Little Guide

- Child Millionaire: **Stock Market Investing for Beginners - How to Build Wealth the Smart Way for Your Child**

- Christian Living: 2 Books with Bonus Content

- **Beginners Quick Guide to Passive Income: Learn** Proven Ways to Earn Extra Income **in the Cyber World**

- **Taming the Tongue: The Power of Spoken Words**

- The Power of **Positive Affirmations**: Each Day a New Beginning